To those

who have gone

before us

INTRODUCTION

This small book is intended as a journey, an exploration into spiritual realms. I invite you to undertake it in the spirit of scientific inquiry. I ask you to experiment with these prayers and declarations and to record for yourself the results you observe in your life and in your consciousness.

Heart Steps is grounded in ancient spiritual tradition. You are asked to "speak the word." In other words, this book is intended not merely to be read, but to be read aloud. (For this reason, I have made an audiotape combining the words of this book with the powerful music of my creative partner, Tim Wheater.)

"In the beginning was the Word," Scripture tells us. The ancients sang the world into existence, Aboriginals believe. Ethiopians believe that the world and God Himself were created by God speaking His own name. In Hopi belief, it was Spider Woman who sang the world into existence—one word at a time. Indians believe, "*Nada Brahma:* the world is sound." As even this brief scan suggests, it is difficult to find a spiritual tradition that does not emphasize the creative power of the word. From the Lakota songs of North America to the song lines crossing Australia, spiritual seekers have always used language—sound—as a safe haven. It is a stairway to higher consciousness as well. I do not ask you to believe this. Instead, I ask you to experiment and see for yourself whether this is true.

The tone of these prayers may at first startle you. These are declarative prayers. They do not beseech divine help, they assume it. These are not the prayers of a sinful, fallen nature begging for release. These are prayers spoken with confidence as children of the

Universe. These prayers claim our birthright. They acknowledge and expand our co-creative bond with a power greater than ourselves. They are not the prayers of exile. They are the prayers of reunion, renewal, and return. God is not "dead." God is not absent from our world. Our consciousness of God is what is missing. "Conscious contact" is what these prayers are all about.

In 1979, composer Billy May gave me a small book of prayers, *Creative Ideas,* by Dr. Ernest Holmes.

"These have worked for me," Billy said.

"Worked?"

"They clear the way."

At the time we were talking, I was newly sober and wondering just how to "let" myself be creative without alcohol as a crutch or a reward.

"I think of it like this," Billy continued. "If you're working on a project and you have a hundred creative horses, you want all of them with you. Now, if thirty of your horses are worried about money, and thirty of your horses are worried about the way the project will be received, you only have another forty to do the creative work at hand. These prayers help you to gather your horses."

With that, he handed me the tiny book.

What a revolution that tiny book caused in my life and in my thinking! I had never read prayers like those, prayers spoken with the confident assurance that God, or "Mind," was deeply, personally interested and interactive in our lives—if we would just speak the word that opened the door that opens the heart.

From 1979 until now, I have worked with—and played with—the power of the positive word. I have found the techniques in this book not merely enlivening or empowering, but actually "healing." They have given me a creative life.

Julia Cameron

HEART
STEPS

The power of the word
is real whether or not
you are conscious of it.

Your own words are the
bricks and mortar of the
dreams you want to realize.
Behind every word flows energy.

SONIA CHOQUETTE

THE UNIVERSE RESPONDS TO MY DREAMS AND NEEDS

There is a unity flowing through all things. This unity is responsive to our needs. Unity responds and reacts to our positive spoken word. We are co-creative beings working with—and within—a larger whole. We embrace and contain this Source, which embraces and contains us. Drawing upon this Inner Source, we have an unlimited supply.

Through the act of affirmative
prayer the limitless resources
of the Spirit are at my command.
The power of the Infinite
is at my disposal.

ERNEST HOLMES

I HAVE THE POWER TO
RECEIVE GREAT ABUNDANCE

I open myself to a more abundant flow. I source myself in the Universe and recognize that the Universe is unlimited in its abundance. I allow myself to receive abundance as a show of the power of God working through me. I allow my life to be made abundant and rich as an example that the power of God can make life abundant and rich. I accept increased flow as proof of God's power. I am receptive soil for God's gardening hands.

THE DREAMS OF MY HEART
ARE THE DREAMS OF
THE UNIVERSE DREAMING
THROUGH ME

I am a gate for God to accomplish great things. Through me and with me, new Life enters the world. I am a portal, an entryway for the grace and power of God to show themselves in the world. As I move toward my fulfillment, God moves toward fulfillment. I am a particle and an article of faith. As I accept the power of God within me, I manifest that power in the world. What I desire is good and what I make is good. My creative nature brings blessings to me and to my world.

Our worst fear is not that we are inadequate, our deepest fear is that we are powerful beyond measure.

NELSON MANDELA

THE GREAT CREATOR CREATES THROUGH ME

We are ourselves creations. We are meant to continue creativity by being creative ourselves. This is the God-force extending itself through us. Creativity is God's gift to us. Using creativity is our gift back to God. It is the natural extension of our creative nature to manifest our dreams. Our dreams come from a divine source. Moving in the direction of our dreams moves us toward our divinity.

Many people pray and receive
the answer to their prayers,
but ignore them—or deny them,
because the answers didn't come
in the expected form.

SOPHY BURNHAM

THE UNIVERSE WATCHES
OVER ME WITH CARE

I am a beloved child of God. The Universe is my home. I am safe and protected in all places, at all times. There is no harm or danger in which my well-being is not provided for. I accept guidance, guardianship in all areas of my life. There is no venture I undertake, no plan or project I conceive which is not shepherded safely. I consciously and daily invoke the protective guidance of God. I receive this guidance within and from people and situations I encounter. I am gently, safely led.

I AM LUMINOUS AND SAFE
IN MY VULNERABILITY

Life requires vulnerability. I treat myself gently and allow myself to be vulnerable. I accept myself as I am today without the need for perfection. I allow myself the freedom to learn without grandiose expectations. I am a living being. I allow my life to flow more broadly across the plain of experience. I allow my life to rest in the sun of self-acceptance.

There are unknown forces within nature;
when we give ourselves wholly to her,
without reserve, she leads them to us;
she shows us those forms which
our watching eyes do not see,
which our intelligence does not
understand or suspect.

AUGUSTE RODIN

ALL CREATURES ARE
DIVINE IN ORIGIN

All creatures are my brothers and sisters. All life exists in God. There is no hierarchy, only harmony. There is a right place for each of us. Each is an important part of the web of Life. Not one of us is dispensable. All are valued. All are important. I am a valued and important part of the web of Life. The web of Life is a valued and important part of me.

ALL OF LIFE IS
MY MENTOR

I honor the wisdom of Life. I learn from Life in all its forms. The tree teaches me. The sparrow and the wren sing my song. I am open to the lessons Life brings to me from the earth. I learn from the wind, from the sun, from the small flowers, and from the stars. I walk without arrogance. I learn from all I encounter. I open my mind and my heart to the guidance and love that come to me from the natural world.

All is procession; the
universe is a procession
With measured and beautiful motion.

WALT WHITMAN

THOSE WHO LOVE ME
COME TO MY SIDE

As I ask for loving companions on my journey, I am led heart to heart and hand to hand to a friendlier world. As I extend my heart and my hand, the world meets me with open arms. As I reach for my wisdom and my compassion to aid others, others respond to me in kind. I am not alone. I am not unseen, unheard, a stranger in the world. As I hold myself a friend among friends, friendship finds me. As I hold myself a lover of Life,

Life responds to me with love. In all times of sorrow and anxiety, I comfort myself through comforting the world. Through cherishing Life, I allow Life to cherish me.

Men cannot live without mystery.
He has a great need of it.

LAME DEER

I LOVE WITH DIVINE
ENERGY AND WISDOM

The face of love is variable. I am able to love without demanding that my relationships assume the structures and forms I might choose for them. My love is fluid, flexible, committed, creative. My love allows people and events to unfold as they need. My love is not controlling. It does not dictate or demand. My love allows those I love the freedom to assume the forms most true to them. I release all those I love from my preconceptions of their path. I allow them the dignity of self-definition while I offer them a constant love that is ever variable in shape.

I DRAW TO ME TRUE LOVE

I draw to myself my right partner, the soul whose love serves my soul's highest potential, the soul whom my soul enhances to highest potential. I draw this partner to me freely and lovingly as I am drawn to this partner. I choose and am chosen out of pure love, pure respect, and pure liberty. I attract one who attracts me equally. I seek and am found. We are a match made in heaven to better this earth.

I LOVE AND AM LOVED
FULLY AND FREELY

My desire to love and be loved is a healthy part of my human nature. Giving and receiving love are as natural as breathing out and breathing in. I breathe in the love I need from Source, which is within me and all around me. I breathe out the love others need. I am nurtured both by giving and by receiving. I freely allow others to love me. I myself freely love others.

MY HEART EXPLORES
THE WORLD WITH WONDER

Life is an adventure. I am an explorer. The world I experience lies within me. The adventures I undertake are within me as well as in the world. I am wonderful and mysterious. I have depths and heights which are beautiful and expansive. As the world is magnificent, so am I. We are one Life, one substance, one growth moving toward fuller love. As I open my heart to the adventure of living, my horizons broaden and my path becomes clear.

The idea is like a blueprint,
it creates an image of the form,
which then magnetizes and guides
the physical energy to flow into that
form and eventually manifests
it on the physical plane.

SHAKTI GAWAIN

I AM A MAGNET FOR GOOD

I attract to myself what I need to grow and expand. As a plant attracts physical nutrients, I attract spiritual nutrients. I attract people, things, and experiences which enhance my potential. I am a magnet for good. I draw to myself love, abundance, creativity, and opportunity. I radiate love, abundance, creativity, and opportunity for others.

The position of the artist is humble.
He is essentially a channel.

PIET MONDRIAN

LIFE ADVANCES THROUGH MY ATTITUDES AND ACTIONS

L ife extends itself through Life. I am a channel for Life to expand and flourish. I am a branch reaching to the sun. As I reach my full potential, I aid and enhance all of Life. My good is good for everyone. My growth is growth for everyone. As I advance, we advance. The Universe moves through me. I move through the Universe. There is harmony, grace, and power in my unfolding.

One of the first things to do is learn
to accept, and to expect this Power to
flow through everything we do.

ERNEST HOLMES

MY CREATIVITY
IS DIVINE IN ORIGIN.
HUMAN IN FORM

L ife is energy, pure creative energy. This energy
is the source of all I desire, all I need, all I
want. When I call upon this source to supply
me, I am freed from depending on people, institutions,
and hierarchies. My good comes to me from all directions, from all quarters. No one person can block my
good. No circumstance can circumvent me. There are
ways and means for God to reach me beyond my imag-
ining. I ask God directly to supply my needs. I listen
for guidance and expect support in all I undertake.

· 17 ·

Why should we all use our creative power . . . ? Because there is nothing that makes people so generous, joyful, lively, bold and compassionate, so indifferent to fighting and the accumulation of objects and money.

BRENDA UELAND

MY HEART IS RECEPTIVE TO THE PROMPTINGS OF SPIRIT

I am attentive to the guidance unfolding in my life. I am alert to promptings from within and without. I act in the world and I allow the world to act also in my affairs. I expect a responsive Universe to react and respond to me. As I become clear and focused for good, my world becomes clear and focused for good. I am a creator engaged in a creative relationship with the world within me and around me. As I create my inner world, my outer world responds in kind. As I establish peace, prosperity, and joy within my heart, these things are manifest in my outer reality.

It is in the knowledge of the
genuine conditions of our lives
that we must draw our strength to
live and our reasons for living.

SIMONE DE BEAUVOIR

MY SOUL IS SUREFOOTED
ON ITS PATH

alance is the key to my serenity. I attain balance by listening to my inner wisdom and to the wisdom of others. There is no situation in which I cannot find a point of balance. There is no circumstance in which I cannot find inner harmony. As I ask to be led into equilibrium and clarity, I will find that my answers come to me. I am wiser than I know, more capable of right action and attitudes than I yet believe. In every event, I seek the balance point of God's action through me.

All nature is alive, awake and
aware with the Divine Presence,
and everything in life responds
to the song of the heart.

ERNEST HOLMES

MINE IS AN
ADVENTUROUS HEART

I choose an expansive life. I choose adventure, freedom, self-expression. I choose self-definition,
self-love, self-renewal. Life expands or contracts
according to my expectations. I expect good and that is
what I experience. Viewing the whole, I choose to be
interconnected yet independent. I allow the God-force
within me to open and enlarge my lens of perception
and realm of action. My horizons stretch ever wider as
I define my identity in terms of my divinity. I am an

adventurer, an explorer, a dreamer whose dreams become true. I embrace the adventure of life. I have courage.

THE UNIVERSE GIFTS
ME WITH COURAGE

I am courageous. I allow the Universe to strengthen and support me as I face difficult, demanding, and dangerous situations. I accept universal help, universal protection, universal guidance. I respond with calm bravery to perilous times, knowing the power of God works through me, so what have I to fear? God protects me. God surrounds me. God is within me. I am without fear.

No man is born into the world
whose work is not born with him.

JAMES RUSSELL LOWELL

MY GOOD IS POWERFUL
AND CANNOT BE STOPPED

There is no outer block to my highest good. No person, situation, event, or misfortune can block the flow of good to me. The flow of good is within me. All things work toward the good. As I allow love to come to me, I am fulfilling my true nature. I am listening to the voice within me which says, "Grow, blossom, this love is nutrition for your true nature." I accept love as I accept the sunshine, the moistening rain. It is natural. I need only receive it.

MY HEART IS CERTAIN
OF ITS GOOD

I am optimistic. I choose to believe and expect the emergence of the best. I enjoy the day I am given and I eagerly anticipate the future. I am alert to negative thinking and I do not allow it to cloud my perceptions. Knowing the unstoppable power of God, I am realistic about people and events but I am optimistic about positive outcomes, positive change. I invite actualizing grace to enter and act in all my affairs, alchemizing difficulty into opportunity.

I AM LARGER
THAN MY PAIN

All loss is a doorway. All pain is an entrance. All suffering is a gate. The Universe is large enough to hold my pain and comfort me. I am small enough to be held and cherished, rocked and soothed. I am large enough to hold compassion, large enough to hold peace. I am united with all through my suffering and through my joy. I connect to my emotions and I connect to others through their emotions. I am both the mountain and the cloud. Circumstances vary, situations change, but I remain rooted in the soil of God. The Universe consoles me and makes me whole.

MY DIGNITY IS SACRED
AND SELF-CONTAINED

I hold my value, honor, and dignity regardless of circumstances. I do not allow the thoughtless or unwarranted behavior of others to cause me to doubt or forget my own worth. In all times of stress and opposition, I ground myself by the spiritual truth that I am divinely sourced, protected, and cherished. I know and affirm that all things work toward my ultimate good through God's grace. I recognize there is no circumstance immune to the power of God. I ask divine intervention in my troublesome affairs. I expect and receive divine intervention and solution. I receive direct and active help.

If the world is to be healed
through human efforts, I am
convinced it will be by ordinary
people, people whose love for
this life is even greater than
their fear. People who can open
to the web of life that called us
into being, and who can rest in
the vitality of that larger body.

JOANNA MACY

THE UNIVERSE FUNDS ME
WITH STRENGTH

In times of adversity, I remember I am strong enough to meet the challenges of my life. I am equal to every situation, a match for every difficulty. Sourced in the power of the Universe, I allow that power to work through me. I meet calamity with strength. I have stamina. Rather than draw on limited resources, I draw on the infinite power within me that moves through me to accomplish its good. I am fueled by all the love, all the strength there is. Loving strength melts mountains. I am ever partnered and supplied by universal flow. Knowing this, I do not doubt my strength. I am strong and secure.

MY SPIRIT
IS LARGE ENOUGH
FOR ANY CIRCUMSTANCE

I am enough. I have wisdom enough. I have faith enough. I know enough. I do not need to strive or strain. I do not need to reach or worry. I am enough. I allow the Universe to act through me. The Universe is more than enough. And so am I.

MY SOUL
IS RICH BEYOND
MY KNOWING

I honor the creator within me. I carry riches, jewels, and abundance. I have a bountiful heart. I am dowried by love, by compassion, by companionship. I act with generosity. I am sourced in God. All goodness flows to me and through me. There is no limit to what I can accomplish. I am the hand of Life flowing toward greater Life. My creations are the creations of the creator within me. I create with freedom and power. I create with bliss and excitement. Through me and in me, the powers of the Universe move to expansion. I am within that power, expanded by that power. It is within me and is expanded through me. As the Universe is powerful and good, so, too, am I.

Expect your every need to be met,
expect the answer to every problem,
expect abundance on every level,
expect to grow spiritually.

EILEEN CADDY

GOD IS THE ROOT OF
MY ABUNDANT SECURITY

S ourced by the Universe, I am able to be generous. I am rooted in the wealth of God as a tree
in rich soil. I share with others from God's un-
ending abundance. As I share, I am replenished. There
is no lack, no shortfall, only flow. I trust and affirm
there is enough—more than enough—for all of us. As
I share God's abundance, my flow increases. As I cele-
brate my increased flow, opportunities and occasions
for still greater generosity appear to me, presenting

themselves as opportunities for my extended faith. Trusting that I am a channel for universal flow, I allow good and abundance to move through me, prospering others and myself. As I prosper others, I am prospered in return.

I AM PART
OF A GREATER WHOLE
AND IT IS A PART
OF ME

I open my mind and my heart to the plan of service which yields joy for me and others. I accept my guidance and direction as they unfold within me. I undertake actions which empower and embody my guidance. I release others from my agendas, trusting completely that the perfect people and events arise for me as I follow my own path.

Now join your hands and with
your hands your hearts.

WILLIAM SHAKESPEARE

I CELEBRATE
THE FULFILLMENT OF
CREATIVE SERVICE

I find joy in service. I open my mind and my heart to the plan of service that brings the most joy to me and to others. I accept my guidance and direction as they unfold within me. Moved by my inner wisdom, I undertake actions which empower and embody my guidance. Moving forward as I am inwardly directed, I release others from my agendas, trusting completely that the perfect people and events will arise to meet me as I follow my path.

This we know: All things
  are connected
like the blood which unites
  one family.
All things are connected.
Whatever befalls the earth
befalls the sons of the earth.
Man did not weave the
  web of life.
He is merely a strand of it.
Whatever he does to the web
He does to himself.

CHIEF SEATTLE

I EMBRACE THE
APPETITES OF LIFE

L ife is tender and rapacious. Everything is fuel
for further Life. Further growth. Nothing which
I experience counts for nothing. Everything—
all joy, all loss, all grief, all grace—is an ingredient in

the greater self which I am building. I am not alone. All sense of loneliness is a forgetting. When I remember that I am a part of Life and Life is a part of me, I am comforted. I see my value. I experience my worth. I allow the Universe to touch me with compassion, to cradle me with love. I am held by the web of Life which I hold dear.

THE EARTH
AND I
ARE ONE LIFE

This earth is made from God. God is made from this earth. There is one substance, one nature, one energy which flows through all and is all. I am a part of this greater whole. This greater whole is a part of me. I am larger than I know.

MY HEART OPENS
TO ALLOW
MY DEEPEST GOOD

Acceptance, openness, allowing are the keys to manifestation. I do not need to will my good. I need to accept my good. I do not need to will my being loved. I need only accept my being loved. I open my heart to accept and allow the good which I desire. I open my heart to accept and allow the love which I desire. I am in God and God is in me. As I yearn for God, I yearn for my own true nature. As I ask God to fulfill me, I ask that I fulfill myself. There is no distance, no need to please and cajole, whimper or manipulate. It is the pleasure of the entire Universe to expand as it desires. My desires are the desires of the Universe. They are fulfilled by the Universe acting through me, toward me.

MY NOURISHMENT COMES
FROM MANY SOURCES

I open myself to abundance from all quarters. I open myself to nourishment and to love. I receive my good in many forms, through many people. I accept my good in all the multiple costumes and disguises which it may undertake. My good comes to me as people, as events and opportunities. My good comes to me as wise counsel, as friendship, as passion and delight. I honor my good by recognizing its many forms. I am grateful and attentive to the abundant good of Life.

*We will discover the nature of our
particular genius when we stop
trying to conform to our own or to
other people's models, learn to be
ourselves, and allow our natural
channel to open.*

SHAKTI GAWAIN

LOYALTY IS MY GIFT
AND MY NATURE

I am loyal to myself and others. I am true to what I believe in and I am true to whom I believe in. My values are grounded in spiritual principles. I place principles before personalities. I do not shape my loyalties to fit convenience. The bedrock of my life is valuing what I know to be real and true. On this I stake all else: that each of us contains divinity, that each of us is worthy of respect, that each of us carries a birthright of dignity and honor. Knowing this, I find loyalty easy, even effortless. Grounded in my own divinity, I am true to what I know to be the truth.

We are the flow, we are the ebb.

We are the weavers; we are the web.

SHEKINAH MOUNTAINWATER

I CELEBRATE THE COMMUNION OF EQUAL HEARTS

I honor the equal wisdom of all souls. I listen for my own guidance and grant to all souls the same dignity. I trust that as I listen, I am properly led. I trust that as others listen, they, too, are led properly and perfectly for the highest good of all.

You must learn to be still in
the midst of activity and to be
vibrantly alive in repose.

INDIRA GANDHI

MY TEMPERAMENT AND
TEMPO ARE ATTUNED TO
THE UNIVERSAL FLOW

I surrender my anxiety and my sense of urgency. I
allow God to guide me in the pacing of my life. I
open my heart to God's timing. I release my dead-
lines, agendas, and stridency to the gentle yet often
swift pacing of God. As I open my heart to God's un-
foldings, my heart attains peace. As I relax into God's
timing, my heart contains comfort. As I allow God to
set the tone and schedule of my days, I find myself in
the right time and place, open and available to God's
opportunities.

I EMBRACE
THE MOMENT

I am fluid and spontaneous. I react and respond openly and easily to the changing face of life. I am focused yet lighthearted. I bring joy and exuberance to my activities. I draw my energy from Life itself. I am an outlet for the energy of the Universe to promote change, growth, and expansion. As I expand and extend my goals and desires, my energies and stamina expand to encompass them. I fulfill my new potential. Knowing I am sourced in universal power, I respond to life with security, spontaneity, and delight. I am more than enough.

*Today I live in the quiet
joyous expectation of good.*

ERNEST HOLMES

MY SOUL HAS PATIENCE
AND CONTAINMENT

I am patient. I am able to live with ambiguity. I am able to allow situations to evolve and alter. I am able to await outcomes. I tolerate quiet periods of non-knowing while solutions emerge and present themselves. I do not force solutions. I expect the successful working-out of difficulties and differences. My heart is wise. It knows when to act and when non-action is the action to take. I trust my patient heart. I trust the power of my containment.

DEATH IS A DOOR TO
FURTHER LIFE

Life intends Life. There is no death that is not another life beginning. There is no end that does not start anew. In every loss, in every grief, there is the hand of comfort, the hand of faith, waiting to move me forward into new ways. I accept the new dominions that come to me through loss. I open my heart to the great and subtle grace that is beginning. All that has gone before, I carry in my heart. My own heart is carried by Life, by love, by the past moving through me, present in me, as it dreams toward the future. I open my heart to the guidance of those I have not lost.

Jump.

JOSEPH CAMPBELL

I
HAVE
AN INNER
COMPASS

I seek help and guidance in all things. I hear my guidance clearly and respond to it with attention. I am free to choose and free to honor my choices. I act with faith and freedom, moving to express that which is God within me. As I open my life to God's guiding care, my life is transformed.

THE UNIVERSE IS IN
CONSTANT CONTACT FOR
MY WELL-BEING

I open my mind and heart to guidance from the Universe. I am open to guidance in all its many forms. I accept help from the Universe through people, events, and places which inspire and instruct me. I listen to the song of Life played through many instruments—through children, animals, the wind, a bird, a flash of sunlight sparkling off glass. All things speak my language. I listen to all languages with my heart. My heart hears higher and higher frequencies of guidance as I raise my own thoughts to the possibility of higher realms guiding and embracing my own.

MY PERCEPTIONS ARE
ACUTE AND ACCURATE

In times of doubt, I remind myself that my sensitivity is acute. I am alert and perceptive. I know—and notice—what I need to know. I register people and events accurately. My antennae are subtle and keen. Denial does not block my perceptions. I am accurate and intuitive. I am shrewd, knowledgeable, sensitive, and clear. Appearances do not deceive me. I sense the truth, respond accurately to reality. I am precisely in tune with my environment. I am grounded and safe. I am sensitive and secure. I am secure because of my sensitivity. It is a divine asset and I use it well.

The real voyage of discovery consists
not in seeking new landscapes,
but in having new eyes.

MARCEL PROUST

MY VISION
IS CLEAR-EYED
AND LONGSIGHTED

I choose reality over denial. I choose clarity over fear. I choose to allow my full potential for clear, grounded thought and action to emerge. I accept divine guidance in its many forms. Guided and clear, I act in my own behalf for my own good and the highest good of others.

MY SOUL IS A COMPASSIONATE HEART

I am compassionate. I allow my heart and imagination to embrace the difficulties and concerns of others. While maintaining my own balance, I find it within myself to extend sympathy, attention, and support. When they are grieved, I listen with openness and gentle strength. I offer loyalty, friendship, and human understanding. Without undermining or enabling, I aid and assist others to find their strength. I allow the healing power of the Universe to flow through me, soothing the hearts and feelings of those I encounter.

*I cannot believe that the inscrutable
universe turns on an axis of
suffering; surely the strange beauty
of the world must somewhere
rest on pure joy!*

LOUISE BOGAN

MY HEART
IS A VESSEL FOR
TENDERNESS. A BALM
IN DIFFICULTY

I am compassionate toward myself about my own vulnerability. I am tender toward myself in all difficult and challenging times. I accept that I have human limits and human emotions, which I honor and attend to. I allow the Universe to comfort me as I open my eyes and heart to difficult realities.

I AM A HEALER
AND MY LOVE
IS MEDICINE

Love is the greatest medicine. I ask to be healing medicine for others. I ask my heart to expand its boundaries and to love others as they wish to be loved. I ask my heart to expand its boundaries and open to my being loved as I wish to be loved.

One day, it was suddenly
revealed to me that everything
is pure spirit.

RAMAKRISHNA

BODY AND SOUL
ARE ONE

There is no separation between body and soul,
spirit and matter. One essence, one unity, runs
through all of life. This essence, the God-
force, is completely pure, completely perfect. I claim
for myself the health and perfection of this divine
force. My body is beautiful, sacred, and beloved. Spirit
infuses my body with radiant goodness. I experience
vitality, enthusiasm, energy, and power. My physical
nature and my spiritual nature are one and the same.
My body's needs and urges are divine in origin. As I listen to my inner guidance, I move to more and more

perfect health, more and more abundant energy, more and more positive thoughts, feelings, and actions. My physical body is a conduit for my spiritual health to pour forth into the world.

Listen. Make a way for
yourself inside yourself.
Stop looking in the other
way of looking.

RUMI

I AM
A LISTENER
WITH THE EARS
OF MY SOUL

I listen with the ears of my heart. I am alert to the promptings of love. I respond to the call of love. I answer with faith to move out in love. I listen, am guided, and act upon that guidance with the conviction that good is unfolding through me and to me.

FREEDOM AND DIGNITY CHARACTERIZE MY RELATIONSHIPS

I release all souls from my agendas for them. I surrender my control and my opinions of the growth and right actions of others. I recognize and accept that divine guidance is acting within each of us. I allow others to script their lives and their dealings with me according to their needs and guidance.

We were born to make manifest
the glory of God within us.

NELSON MANDELA

CREATIVITY
IS MY BIRTHRIGHT

I am a natural creator. Creativity is the natural order of life. Life is energy—pure creative energy. It
is my birthright to co-create my life and my experience. My dreams come from God. The power to fulfill my dreams is God given. There is an indwelling,
underlying creative power infusing all of life, including
ourselves. When we open ourselves to our creativity,
we open ourselves to the Great Creator working with
us and within us.

*Every child is an artist. The
problem is how to remain an
artist once he grows up.*

PABLO PICASSO

MY HEART IS A GARDEN
FOR CREATIVE IDEAS

I recognize that art begins in the heart. I love my creative nature and I love expressing it. I create as an act of love and connection. I allow the Universe to dream through me, to act through me, to create through me.

MY LIFE IS AT
THE CENTER OF
GOD'S CONSCIOUSNESS

There is no distance in the heart of God. There is no separation. I am in the center of my good. It is unfolding where I am and everywhere. At all times, at all places, I—and everyone—are in the heart of God. There is no leaving God. There is no being left. When I feel most alone, I am still held safely. When I am most afraid, I am still protected. All events, however painful, move toward the good.

ALL THAT I CHERISH IS
PRECIOUS TO SPIRIT

All that I love is loved by God. Each person that I cherish is in God's heart. There is no beloved whom God cannot aid. There is no difficulty, no barrier which God cannot dissolve. In the heart of all life is the heart of God. Whoever we are, however we pray, our prayers are heard. I pray with confidence for God to act effectively in the lives of those I love. I trust that situations and opportunities will unfold for them in divine order, leading all to the greatest good.

When we create something, we always
create it first in a thought form.

SHAKTI GAWAIN

I AM EXPERIENCE
EXPANDING

I am born and breathe life into Life. I experience and I expand experience. Consciously and creatively I realize my full human potential. It is larger and wider than my individual vision. As I recognize and commit to my shared humanity, my possibilities and my abilities increase and multiply. Sourced in God, I am miraculous. The miraculous is natural.

I AM AN INSTRUMENT OF
DIVINE CREATION

I offer myself as a channel for higher creativity. I allow the Universe to work through me. I give over my ideas of limitations and potential. I accept an expanded sense of self. I accept an expanded sense of service. I am guided to grow and I accept that growth freely and without reservation. I allow the pattern of God within me to express its fullest form.

We're afraid of feelings. We
rush through our lives searching
yet not living. For those who
have the interest to look closely,
life becomes art.

TIME IS MY FRIEND

My time is expansive and flexible. I have enough time, more than enough time, to accomplish my dreams and my goals. I use my time wisely. I understand the fluidity of time. I pace myself with ease, claiming my right to determine my own tempo and rhythm, velocity and trajectory through life. Time does not rule me. Time does not dominate me. I work with time as a flexible tool. I relish my use of time.

Time is the stuff of which
life is made.

BENJAMIN FRANKLIN

Without discipline, there's
no life at all.

KATHARINE HEPBURN

TIME IS MY PARTNER

It is my choice to use time festively and expansively. I have plenty of time, more than enough time. I fill my time with love, expansion, enthusiasm, exuberance, and commitment. I both act and rest at perfect intervals. Proper use of time comes easily to me. I set the rhythm of my days and years, alert to inner and outer cues which keep me in gentle harmony. Time is my friend and my partner. I let it work for me. I breathe out anxiety and breathe in renewal. I neither fight time nor surrender to time. We are allies as I move through life.

The Holy Spirit is our harpist,
And all strings
Which are touched in Love
Must sound.

MECHTILD OF MAGDEBURG

MY HEART IS A CHANNEL
FOR DIVINE LOVE

I open my heart to love. I invite the love of the Universe to love through me, nurturing myself and others. I receive and I give love in a natural flow. My love is both steady and ever changing, ever responsive. My love is both constant and flexible. As I give love, I feel love. As I seek to love, I am beloved. I cherish myself as fully and as deeply as I cherish others whom I love.

*When we recognize the Divine
Presence everywhere, then we know
that It responds to us and that
there is a Law of Good, a Law of
Love, forever giving of itself to us.*

ERNEST HOLMES

MY HEART KNOWS
ITS PARTNER

I open my heart to receiving the love of my true
and intended mate. I open my heart to giving love
to my true and intended mate. I open to divine
guidance regarding our right relationship. I trust completely that I will recognize and be recognized by the
soul for whom I am a perfect match. I need no artifice,
no ploys, no strategies. My true nature is loving and
that is all that is required by this love.

When you see each leaf as a
separate thing, you can see
the tree, you can see the
spirit of the tree, you can
talk to it, and maybe you can
begin to learn something.

WILLIAM J. RAUSCH

MY ENTIRE BEING
IS ALERT AND ALIVE

I accept the guidance which comes to me in subtle forms. I surrender the arrogance of my intellect and embrace its alert intelligence instead. I allow my mind to listen to my heart. I allow my heart to have a voice in my life choices. I embrace both mind and heart, knowing that in partnership they guide me well. There is no circumstance in which I am abandoned.

There is no place in which I cannot be found. As I listen to first my heart and then my mind, I find that the Universe does speak to me with gentle clarity. A path does emerge on which I walk with safety.

I AM DIVINELY HELPED. GUARDED. AND GUIDED

I am always led, always guided. There is no desert, no grief, no wasteland too devastated for the presence of God to find me. I am beloved. I am cherished and seen. I am always heard. Even when my prayers fall on seeming silence, they are heard. God is with me always. I am in God's presence and God is present in me. If I open to guidance, I am always led, always helped. I can hear the voice of God within me. I can hear the urgings of my soul. When I cry out in anguish as being abandoned, even in that despair, the voice of God whispers within me if I will only listen.

All creation is a manifestation
of the delight of God—God seeing
Himself in form, experiencing Himself
in His own actions, and knowing
Himself in us as us.

ERNEST HOLMES

MY TRUE NATURE IS THE
EXPERIENCE OF UNITY

All separation is fear. All fear is illusion. We forget that we are one. We forget that your joy is my joy. Your pain, my pain. In our unity we have communion, compassion, consolation, communication. In our unity, we are one people, one earth, one song. Each of us sings a True Note. Each of us adds to the chorus. Each of us contains the wisdom, the breadth and the height, to encompass all of us in our full humanity. When we remember who we are, we know there is only union, only hope, only good unfolding for us all. When we remember God with us and us within God, fear drops away. Loneliness passes. Reunion and rejoicing fill my heart.

God knows no distance.

CHARLESZETTA WADDLES

NONE ARE LOST AND
ALL ARE FOUND

There is no place or person beyond the reach of God. As I am in God and God is in me and all people, I directly influence people and events through my creative consciousness. Therefore, in a spirit of cooperation and non-coercion, I claim the highest good for all in every circumstance.

What we need is more people
who specialize in the impossible.

THEODORE ROETHKE

MY HEART
IS A THRONE
FOR COURAGE

Life requires courage. All courage that I need is given me by Life itself. I am guided and supported in every step. I need only open myself to receiving support and guidance. I honor my humility in admitting my need for help. I welcome the dignity of being a fellow among fellows. I honor myself for my courage in following my guidance.

I EXPAND BEYOND
MY FEARS

I relinquish all agendas and timelines originating in my fears. I relinquish all rationalizations and defenses grounded in my fears. I open my heart instead to the healing perspective of compassionate patience for others and myself. I allow myself the luxury of time, the dignity of right action and right timing.

It is life that must be our practice.
It is not enough to hear spiritual
truth or even to have our own
spiritual insights. Every aspect
of what happens to us must become
part of a learning experience.

DIANE MARIECHILD

I AM PARTNERED
BY THE UNIVERSE
IN ALL MY DEALINGS

I lead my life in partnership with the Universe. In all situations I have choices and options which lead me to freedom and expansion. In every time of darkness or difficulty I affirm there is a doorway which will open if I knock. I am never separated from the power of God. There is nothing which stands between me and God. I am within God and God is within me. We are one substance, one energy, one Life.

Over and over, we have to go back
to the beginning. We should not
be ashamed of this. It is good.
It's like drinking water.

NATALIE GOLDBERG

GOD IS ALWAYS WITH ME
AND WITHIN ME

In times of adversity, I accept divine help in my life. I invite, expect, and welcome divine interaction and intervention in my affairs. I recognize there is no circumstance immune to the power of God. I ask and receive divine intervention in my troublesome affairs. I seek and receive direct and active help. I ask for guidance and am assured I receive it. I ask for wisdom, comfort, clarity, and all qualities of which I have need. Because these qualities are within God and God is within me, I always receive my answered prayers.

All substance is energy in motion.
It lives and flows. Money is
symbolically a golden, flowing stream
of concretized vital energy.

THE MAGICAL WORK OF THE SOUL

I AM A KINGDOM OF
RICH RESOURCES

I am abundantly supplied. As I ask, I receive. As I reach inward, Source flows from me outward. There is no lack, no hesitation. I am directly sourced to universal abundance. My needs are met. My wants are supplied. I draw with confidence upon God-source, knowing that it responds to me with immediate and full attention.

MONEY IS A STRONG
CURRENT FLOWING
TO ME AND THROUGH ME
FOR GOOD

Money is a means to an end. It is a servant and not a master. When I ask for money, I am asking for supply. It may come to me as money, but it may also come to me in other forms. I am alert to the many forms my supply may take. While I welcome and receive money as one form, I also welcome and receive supply in all forms it appears.

Inside you there's an artist you
don't know about. . . .
Say yes quickly, if you know, if you've
known it from before the beginning
of the universe.

RUMI

THE UNIVERSE BRINGS
GIFTS TO MY HEART

I allow the Universe to work through me to give me what it desires. I no longer block my good, my expansion, by greedy demands or by stinginess. Instead, I open my heart and mind to prosperous living. I allow myself to be taught how to live generously and abundantly. God is the gardener and I am the soil. I allow God to fructify my life in all ways.

Explore daily the will of God.

C. G. JUNG

MY TRUST EXPANDS

As I trust, I learn to trust more fully. I honor myself for my bravery in taking risks. As I risk, I learn to risk more fully. Life supports my expansion into a larger and more grounded self. I am able to admit mistakes freely and make course adjustments easily. I see myself as a process, a work in progress. I extend compassion for growing pains to myself and to others.

THE EARTH IS
MY WISE TEACHER

I embrace the wisdom of this earth. I accept my own life's seasonality in all things. I embrace my times of apparent dormancy as well as my showier seasons of growth. I trust the quiet times of apparent absence as the necessary gestation time for a fruitful future.

MY FUTURE
BLOSSOMS WITHIN ME

The future is with me now. It is unfolding within me, present and sturdy. My dreams and desires are the seeds of my future. I contain within me everything I need to manifest fully my heart's desires. Since God is within and I am within God, there is no yearning which cannot be satisfied if I will allow its satisfaction. There is no good which cannot come to me if I will allow it to come. It is not necessary for me to "will" the acquisition of some person, event, or situation. I need only align my will to accept the unfolding of my desire.

My physical body is a temple of
the living Spirit which animates it,
rebuilds it after the image of
Its own perfection, and keeps
it in perfect health, harmony,
and wholeness.

ERNEST HOLMES

GOD IS THE GREAT
PHYSICIAN
AND I AM HEALED

I build my physical health upon a spiritual basis. As I turn my attention to the God-force within me, my spiritual health improves, and as it does it strengthens my physical vitality. All sense of strain and exhaustion, all sense of being overwhelmed or fatigued, washes away as I remind myself that God is the source of my energy, the Source of my power. God is the great creator. With God within me, I create radiant good health. I create beauty and serenity within my body. With God within me, I release all negative thoughts and conditions which weaken me physically and spiritually. As I increase my spiritual health, my physical health improves as well. Remembering that my body is a gift from God, I care for it with loving attention and it responds with radiant health.

Today I identify my body with
the action of God, the radiant Life
of the Divine Being. I identify
my physical body with my spiritual
body, claiming they are one and
the same. I know that every aspect
of my body corresponds to the radiant
perfection of the living Spirit.
There is perfection in every part
of my being, perfect wholeness
and completeness.

ERNEST HOLMES

WITH GOD I CREATE FOR
MYSELF RADIANT HEALTH

God is the source of my health, the source of
my healing. There is no condition that cannot be improved through spiritual means. I
am in God. God is within me. My prayers are answered

both internally and externally. As I remember my own divine nature, as I remember the health and radiance that is God's, I strengthen both my body and my soul. As I open to divine aid, divine support, and a consciousness of divine presence within me, my spiritual and physical health is established. I claim for myself divine help, divine health, divine healing.

I AM A PLANNED AND PRECIOUS CHILD OF SPIRIT

I do not walk alone. I am not friendless. I am led, guided, comforted, and consoled. The earth has plans for me. I am loved and valued. My voice is heard My song is a precious note in the symphony of Life. I remember these things and treat myself with dignity. I am tender toward my fears, compassionate toward my pain. I reassure myself with gentleness that I am not abandoned, never unheard or unseen. I ask Life to meet me with Life. I open my heart and my

mind to sign of companionship. I receive friendship
in many forms. I recognize love with its many faces.
I walk in the companionship of loving guides and
guiding love.

THE UNIVERSE
CRADLES MY HEART

I find comfort and support from many sources. I am cradled and caressed by loving forces which guide me to my good. I am able, on ever-deepening levels, to feel safe and protected as I move in the world.

Merely looking at the world
around us is immensely different
from seeing it.

FREDERICK FRANCK

I FIND STRENGTH IN
MY KNOWLEDGE

I trust my clarity. I open myself to know what I need to know to see clearly and accurately in all situations. I accept support for my knowledge from all sources. I allow the Universe to hold me in loving arms as I absorb all proper realizations.

MY CHOICES ARE WISE
AND WELL GUIDED

In times of aimlessness, I find focus by seeking the voice of guidance within me. I listen for the promptings of my heart. I am alert to signs and signals in the world around me. I open my thoughts to receive the guidance that may come to me from strangers. Even in times of blindness, I know that I am guided. When I feel I cannot see or hear, even then I am being led. I am not alone. I am not lost. There is no dark grief that cannot be penetrated by the gentle rain of guidance if I will open my heart.

It is only with the heart that one
can see rightly; what is essential
is invisible to the eye.

<small>ANTOINE DE SAINT-EXUPÉRY</small>

I LIVE IN
LOVING HARMONY

I draw to me persons who have pure and loving hearts, high ideals, deep compassion, and good humor. I manifest myself a pure, loving, and compassionate heart. I love others through God and God loves others through me. I accept friendships founded in this true love. I offer friendship of this truly loving nature. I encounter love in those I meet and those I meet encounter love in me.

I DANCE GRACEFULLY TO THE
TIMING OF THE UNIVERSE

I respond gratefully and lovingly to the differing tempos, actions, and needs of others. Recognizing that we partner each other in a great and subtle dance, I accept their growth and their pace as adding to the subtle music of my life. I accept their choices and their actions as fully as guided and dignified as my own. Living in partnership with Life, I accent correction and expansion through the actions of others. I react with love, faith, and dignity when challenged.

Each one of us has all the
wisdom and knowledge we
ever need right within us.
It is available to us through
our intuitive mind, which
is our connection with
universal intelligence.

SHAKTI GAWAIN

I CHERISH MY
INDIVIDUAL INTEGRITY

I honor my own integrity and the integrity of others. I am guided by love. I allow myself to feel the love that is guiding others. Like the earth, I enjoy seasons of renewal. I forgive shortcomings and failures, arrogance and shortsightedness. I allow such human foibles to be dissolved in the graceful flow of life ongoing. Life is a river which flows through me, washing me clean of judgment, cleansing me with the waters of compassion. I allow life to be both tender and clear. I choose the longer view of wisdom over the more short-lived satisfaction of being "right."

MY HEART IS A VERDANT MEADOW WITH MANY BLOOMS

I open my heart to receiving love and respect. I open my heart to many quarters. I allow my good to come to me from all directions. Remembering that the Universe is my source, I release individuals from any demands that they be the source of my good. I allow the Universe to support me as it chooses, not as I demand. I surrender my narrow vision to a broader and longer view of events. I trust that as I respect and honor myself and others, I will be treated in kind.

I am still learning.

MICHELANGELO

All of the larger-than-life questions
about our presence here on earth
and what gifts we have to
offer are spiritual questions.
To seek answers to these questions
is to seek a sacred path.

DR. LAUREN ARTRESS

THE WATERS OF MY SPIRIT
ARE DEEP AND PURE

I draw from the well of universal experience and consciousness. I replenish that well by putting attentive love and kindness into the world. I respect the unity and connection of all things to one another. I live consciously and creatively as part of a sacred unity.

Here in this body are the sacred rivers:
here are the sun and moon as well as
all the pilgrimage places. . . .
I have not encountered another
temple as blissful as my own body.

SARAHA

I AM A BELOVED CREATURE
PRECIOUS TO THE WORLD

I love and I am beloved. I am an integral part of the web of life. I am connected to all things. All things are connected to me. I claim and experience my interconnected divinity. I experience the inner divinity of all things. As I acknowledge and salute the divinity in me and others, I experience harmony and healthy interdependence. All things move through me and with me toward the good.

I DANCE THE DANCE OF LIFE
IN SPIRITED PARTNERSHIP

I discover correction and expansion through the differences I find with others. I react with love, faith, dignity, and curiosity when challenged. I meet each challenge as an opportunity to explore my strengths and my flexibility. I honor my own autonomy and I honor the autonomy of others. I honor my own desires even as I recognize and honor the desires of others. I acknowledge and respect my similarities and my differences with those with whom I interact. I allow my personal universe to be varied and colorful. I grant myself and all I encounter the dignity of our unique individuality and variable needs.

Every time you don't follow your
own inner guidance, you feel a loss
of energy, loss of power, a sense
of spiritual deadness.

SHAKTI GAWAIN

MY HEART
HOLDS INTEGRITY

I love integrity. I am authentic in my responses to people and events. I respond with dignity and courage from a core belief that I am worthy. My values are worthwhile. My principles are shaped by my inner knowing, not by my external circumstances. I bring to the changing flow of life events an inner steadiness, an inner compass. I am whole and unified in body, mind, and spirit. My integrity is natural.

No matter how imperfect the
appearance may be, or painful
or discordant, there is still
an underlying perfection, an
inner wholeness, a complete and
perfect Life, which is God.

ERNEST HOLMES

MY PHYSICAL HEALTH
RESTS ON
A SPIRITUAL FOUNDATION

My body is the beloved vessel for my spirit. I treat my body with tenderness and gentle respect. I offer my body friendship and support. My body speaks to me of my spirit's needs. When I need rest, my body asks me to refresh my spirit. When I am hungry, my body asks me to nourish myself, body and soul. When I listen to my body's cues and signals, my spiritual path unfolds with clarity and power. Spirit speaks to me through body. We embody our spiritual lives. As I recognize my body as an equal partner to my spirit, my soul strength increases. As the health of my soul becomes radiant and alive, the health of my body takes on new vitality. Body and soul are one life, one essence. I salute them as loving partners. My body and soul live in vibrant harmony.

All sanity depends on this: that
it should be a delight to feel heat
strike the skin, a delight to stand
upright, knowing the bones are
moving easily under the flesh.

DORIS LESSING

THE NATURAL WORLD
IS MY HOME
AND MY HAVEN

I cherish the natural world. I see it in the wisdom of God's unfolding. I surrender my resistance to unfolding fully and beautifully. I embrace the mystery of my own evolution. I invite my divine nature to expand and nurture myself and others.

CREATIVITY IS
MY TRUE NATURE

The refusal to be creative is an act of self-will and is counter to our true nature. When we open to our creativity, we are opening to God: good, orderly direction. As we pursue our creative fulfillment, all elements of our life move toward harmony. As we strengthen our creativity, we strengthen our connection to the Creator within. Artists love other artists. Our relationship to God is co-creative, artist to artist. It is God's will for us to live in creative abundance.

> *God, guard me from those*
>   *thoughts*
> *Men think in the mind alone*
> *He that sings a lasting song*
> *Thinks in the marrow-bone.*

WILLIAM BUTLER YEATS

WE ARE DEEP MUSIC

I am a music waiting to be heard. I am a song unfolding. My notes are the voice of Life singing through me in majesty. I open my throat to the word of creation. I speak my truth and build my life upon it. I open my mouth to exclaim the glory that I feel within me. I give voice to God and God's plan for me. I refuse to be small when God intends for me to be large. I expand without pride, without arrogance. I expand through love. I open my heart and mind to the brighter, clearer, and more joyous vistas Life intends for me. I allow Life to create through me the better life which I speak and see.

I EMBRACE MY
CURRENT REALITY
AND ACKNOWLEDGE
ITS GIFTS

I surrender "if only" agendas for happiness. I find happiness and peace in my current circumstances. I allow goodness to flow to me in every time and in every place. I open to receiving good from any and all sources, at any and all moments. I am alert for my good and I enjoy its many disguised and various forms.

I AM IN RHYTHM
WITH THE FLOW
OF LIFE

I accept divine timing in my life. I surrender control of the tempo of my good's unfolding. I am both eager and patient as my heart is prepared to receive God's gifts of love, friendship, creativity, and abundance. I trust good is coming to pass for me in perfect timing for my highest good.

To be at peace with ourselves,
we need to know ourselves.

CAITLIN MATTHEWS

I
CELEBRATE
MY FULL
HUMANITY

I allow myself to be fully human. I treat myself with loving kindness. I honor and recognize my essential goodness. I honor and recognize my ability to love, to communicate, to share, and to give. I do not have to do any of these things perfectly. There is beauty in the abilities I do have.

Every blade of grass has its Angel
that bends over it and whispers,
"Grow, grow."

THE TALMUD

MY SPIRIT FINDS COMPANIONSHIP IN MANY FORMS

I allow myself to be guided and comforted by the Universe. I allow people and events to gently lead me to my good. I ask for help in all of my affairs and I accept the help that is offered me from many quarters. I do not walk alone. I do not call in vain. Even my whispered dreams are heard by an attentive Universe. I am alert to the help which comes to me for their unfolding.

No more words.
Hear only the voice within.

R U M I

THE
UNIVERSE IS MY
GUIDE AND GUARD

The Universe guides and guards its children. I listen and I hear True Guidance, which moves me into loving expansion. I trust my guidance and I act on it faithfully. I move into new territories knowing the way is prepared for me. I walk in safety. My guidance leads me and I follow it with trust.

The will is meant to guide you . . .
so that whatever is appropriate
to any situation is what you
feel like doing and also do.

CEANNE DEROHAN

MY GUIDANCE
IS WISE AND
TRUSTWORTHY

I embrace the wisdom of my own inner guidance. I embrace the guidance of my own inner wisdom. I trust, too, the inner wisdom and guidance of others. I trust that others are wise and good.

As you grow spiritually your words
gain more power to affect people.

SANAYA ROMAN

MY HEART IS
A HOME FOR LOVE

My heart is a home for love. I open my heart to compassion, to charity, to respect, and to recognition. I encounter those I meet with openness and with respect. I honor the path that each is walking. I salute in all that I encounter the dignity of God. All differences, all difficulties, are noticed but not condemned. I respect the individuality of every soul. I accept our equality and our brotherhood.

THE LOVE IN MY HEART
IS CREATIVE AND
CONSTRUCTIVE

I ask my heart to expand its boundaries and love others as they wish to be loved. I ask my heart to expand its boundaries and open to my being loved as I wish to be loved. I relax my rigid ideas about what love should look like. I open to love's infinite variety. I find love in the face of a flower, love in the glint of sun on a city street. Love walks with me. I carry it in my heart.

INDEX

ABOUT THE AUTHOR

Julia Cameron is an active artist who teaches internationally. A poet, playwright, fiction writer, and essayist, she has extensive credits in film, television, and theater, and is an award-winning journalist. She is the author of the best-selling books on creative practice *The Artist's Way* and *The Vein of Gold*, and for nearly two decades has taught and refined her methods.